The Duck in the Gun

written by Joy Cowley
illustrated by Robyn Belton

For days, the General and his men had been marching. Now they were at the town and ready to fight.

The General called his Gunner. "Is the gun in place?" he asked.

"Yes, sir," said the Gunner.

"Is it aimed at the town?"

"Yes, sir," said the Gunner.

"Good," said the General. "Load it. When I give the order, fire."

"Very well, sir," said the Gunner, and he went away.

But a while later he came back. "Sir, we can't fire the gun."

"Why not?" said the General.

"Because we can't load it, sir."

The General grew red in the face. "Why can't you load it?"

"Please, sir," said the Gunner. "There's a duck in the gun."

"A duck?" shouted the General.

"It has made a nest in it, sir."

"The nerve of it!" shouted the General. "Get rid of it at once!"

"I've tried," said the Gunner, "but the duck won't come out. I think it's sitting on some eggs."

"I'll soon fix it," said the General, picking up his sword. "I'll show that duck it can't stop an army."

4

The General and the Gunner went out to where the gun had been set, aimed at the town.

The General looked down the gun, and saw two small eyes looking back at him. "Here, dilly, dilly, dilly," he called. "Nice dilly."

The duck said quack-quack, but didn't move.

The General's face turned red again.
"Come out, blast you!" he shouted, and he banged
on the gun with his sword.

There was another quack, but the duck did not stir
from her nest.

The General stamped up and down.

"To think that a duck could upset my plans," he said.

"There is something you can do, sir," said one of the men. "You can fire it with the duck inside."

"No, no, no!" said the General. "We'll think of something else. Ah, I know. We'll borrow a gun."

The General put on all his medals. Then he took a white flag and went to the town.

"Take me to your Prime Minister," he said to the town guards.

The guards led him through the streets to the Prime Minister's house. The General knocked on the door. At once, it was opened by the Prime Minister's daughter.

"Good afternoon," said the General. "Do you know who I am?"

"Oh, yes," said the girl. "I've seen your picture in the papers. Won't you come in?" She turned away and called, "Father, here is the General to see you."

"How do you do?" said the Prime Minister.

"Not very well," said the General. Then he told the Prime Minister about the duck in the gun.

"What are you going to do about it?" said the Prime
Minister.

The General coughed and looked at the floor.
"That's why I came to see you. I was wondering if you
could lend us a gun. I mean, it's not very fair if you
have guns and we haven't."

"Oh, I agree," said the Prime Minister. "But you see, we have only one gun."

"Couldn't we share it?" said the General. "You could fire a shot at us; then we could take the gun and fire a shot at you."

The Prime Minister laughed. "Goodness, no! We can't let you have our gun. Besides, it's far too heavy to move."

The General looked unhappy.

"You'll have to put the war off for three weeks," said the Prime Minister. "By that time, the duck will have hatched her eggs, and you will have your gun back."

The General shook hands with the Prime Minister. "That's fair enough," he said. "We'll forget about the war for three weeks."

When the men heard the news, they were very pleased. This meant they would have three weeks' leave. They were so pleased, they put food down the gun whenever the General wasn't looking.

But after one week, the General had another problem. He put on his medals, picked up his white flag, and went to see the Prime Minister again.

"How are you?" asked the Prime Minister.

"Not good at all," said the General. "The truth is, I'm running out of money. For a whole week my men have done nothing, and they expect to be paid for it."

"That is a problem," said the Prime Minister.

"I don't suppose you could lend me some money," said the General.

"No," said the Prime Minister. "I can't give men money for doing nothing. But I can pay them if they will work for me. See our town? It needs painting. The houses are shabby and the shops look a mess. In two weeks, your men could paint the whole town."

"What a great idea!" said the General. "Thanks very much. I'll tell my men at once."

This time the men were not so pleased. But when the General said he could no longer pay them, they agreed to work in the town.

Early next morning, they put on old clothes and left the camp.

The General went out to look at the gun. The duck was still there, sitting on her nest and quacking to herself. The General looked over his shoulder to make sure he was alone. He took some cake from his pocket, put it quickly down the gun, and then went back to his tent. He spent the rest of the day reading and lying in the sun.

Every day, the men went to work in the town. The camp was very quiet. Sometimes the General would look at the town through his glasses and watch it change hue.

Sometimes he visited the Prime Minister and his daughter and drank tea in their garden. Sometimes he would just walk as far as the gun, with a pocketful of bread or biscuits.

Near the end of the third week, the eggs hatched. The General went past the gun. He heard not only quack-quack-quack, but also a tiny peep-peep-peep.

The General rang the alarm bell as loudly as he could. At once, the men put down their paint and brushes and ran back to camp.

"Attention!" called the General.
"The duck's eggs have hatched."
He looked inside the gun. "Here,
dilly, dilly," he called.

Out popped a little head. It was
the first duckling.

Very carefully, the General lifted it to the ground. Then another duckling came out, and another, until there were eight of them waddling around the General's feet. Last out was the mother duck. She looked at all the men and quacked loudly. Then she flew down to her ducklings and marched them off across the grass.

"Three cheers for the duck," shouted the men, throwing their hats in the air. "Hooray, hooray, hooray!"

"Now we can use our gun again," said the General. "Now we can have the war."

The men stopped cheering. They became very quiet. They stood with their hats in their hands and looked down at the ground.

"Please, sir," said the Gunner. "We can't shoot at that town. We would spoil the new paint."

"Yes," said the other men. "We've worked for two weeks on those houses."

The General nodded. It did seem silly to blow up freshly painted houses. Besides, he had become rather fond of the Prime Minister's daughter.

"What will we do then?" he said.

"You couldn't put the war off for good, could you, sir?" said the Gunner. "After we've finished painting the town, we can all go home."

The General thought for a long time. "All right," he said. "I'll go and tell the Prime Minister."

So that was the end of the war.

The men finished the painting, and the General
married the Prime Minister's daughter. It was a big
wedding with flowers and a cake that had a white
sugar gun on top.

And, of course, the duck came.

She and her eight ducklings were there to march behind the army band.